What NOT to Do at Work!

What NOT to Do at Work!
Copyright © 2005 Sweetwater Press
Produced by Cliff Road Books

Printed in The United States of America

ISBN: 1-58173-408-5

This work is a compilation from numerous sources. Every effort has been made to ensure accuracy. However, the publisher cannot be responsible for incorrect information.

What NOT to Do at Work!

Compiled and Edited by
Linda J. Beam

SWEET
WATER
PRESS

About the Author

Linda J. Beam holds a B.A. in English from Judson College, and an M.A. in English from the University of Alabama at Birmingham. Her extensive editorial experience includes work with medical journals and textbooks, and a variety of corporate publications. In addition, she has developed and presented business communication seminars on business writing, and basic grammar and punctuation. She currently works as Managing Editor at Crane Hill Publishers in Birmingham, Alabama. Her other publications include *What NOT to Say!, What NOT to Name Your Baby!, What NOT to Do in Polite Company!,* and *What's Your Bible I.Q.?*

Contents

Tripping Over Pebbles

I read a quote recently that said, "Nobody trips over mountains. It is the small pebble that causes you to stumble." How true this is in the workplace! Most people are capable of handling their jobs overall, or they wouldn't have been hired in the first place. But they find very often that it's the small things that trip them up, create uncomfortable situations, and just plain cause problems.

The large number of people who attend business etiquette seminars and classes is proof that people want to learn to do the right thing. After all, many of them spend more time at work than they do at home. Their colleagues become their secondary family. But as they grow accustomed to working with each other every day, they begin to take each other for granted, and very often "forget to remember" proper workplace etiquette.

It is precisely because we do spend so much time working, and because the people we work with are valued parts of our lives, that manners must be remembered and observed. The ability to get along with others, to do the right thing at the right time, and in the right way, are important things to know, and make a good employee a valuable one as well. A recent survey underscored the importance of courtesies in the workplace by finding that soft skills are more important in the workplace than actual business skills.

Good manners not only provide a way to deal appropriately with routine office matters, they also help employees know how to act with people representing a variety of mindsets, cultures, and genders. Business etiquette assures that business is conducted smoothly regardless of differences.

What NOT to Do at Work! identifies the fine points, the "pebbles," that await us in the office. It will smooth the way for you to be the courteous co-worker that you want to be.

First Day on the Job:
Rules for Rookies

First Day on the Job:
Rules for Rookies

The first day of a new job has been compared to the first day of school: you have to meet new people and get new supplies. But this is an exciting time, too, with nothing but possibility ahead of you. Whether it is your first day of working at all, or your first day of a new job, make the most of it by remembering some basic workplace rules.

What NOT to Do

- Do not be late for your first day.

- Do not run out the door right at quitting time.

- Do not dress provocatively, or too trendy.

- Do not make snap judgments about who is nice or who is important. You will probably change your mind about some of your first impressions.

- Do not form alliances too quickly. You don't know on the first day who the office gossip is, or the company pariah. Let relationships develop over time.

Talk about a bad start! On his first day with the Yankees, superstar pitcher Randy Johnson shoved a cameraman out of his way, yelling, "Get out of my face, that's all I ask." He later sheepishly apologized by saying, "Obviously I feel very foolish today at such a great moment of my career that I would have to stand before you and apologize for my actions."

First Day on the Job: Rules for Rookies

- Do not say, "That's not how we did it at my old company."

- Do not watch the clock.

- Do not listen to or participate in office gossip.

- Do not spend a lot of time with personal phone calls. It's only natural that your friends or family might call to see how things are going, and to wish you well, but make even those calls brief.

- Do not talk about your former employer. If you talk about how wonderful he or she was, people will wonder why you didn't just stay there. If you speak badly about your previous situation, you will sound bitter.

- Do not overreact. Mistakes are bound to happen, and everyone knows there will be a learning curve for any new employee.

- Do not ask personal questions about people in the office.

> **Typical first-day-of-work blunders by new employees include forgetting the name of the person who interviewed them, answering the phone with the name of their former employer, and getting lost in the building.**

- Do not divulge too much information about yourself too quickly. This may seem pushy to some people.

- Do not forget to say "Thank you" when co-workers take their time to help you learn the ropes.

First Day on the Job: Rules for Rookies

What to Do

- Take a look at the research you did on the company during the job interview process. Review what the company does and vital information about it.

- Dress appropriately. You should have learned about the company's dress code during the interview, but if not, dress conservatively until you figure out the norm.

- Arrive at least fifteen minutes before your starting time. Do not arrive too early or you could disrupt the schedule of the person training you.

- Smile!

- Be ready to work.

- Have a positive attitude.

- Be polite to everyone from the receptionist to the janitor.

- Introduce yourself to people as you meet them.

- Try to learn co-workers' names quickly.

- Listen and learn; observe and ask questions instead of trying to impress others with how much you know.

> **Surveys show that over three-fourths of office workers rank the first day of a new job as one of the most unnerving of their adult lives.**

- Review with your boss what you already know about your function and position.

First Day on the Job:
Rules for Rookies

- Find out what needs to be done immediately.

- Ask questions about anything you don't understand.

- Carry a pad to jot down important information that you learn throughout the day.

- Find out the locations of the basics: restrooms, coffee machine, copier, and printer.

- Ask about guidelines for computer use: Can you get personal e-mails? Can you access the Internet for personal use on a limited basis?

- Watch your language. Avoid profanity and suggestive remarks.

- Demonstrate a willingness to learn new things.

> **"We're supposed to be perfect our first day on the job and then show constant improvement."**
>
> Ed Vargo, Major
> League Baseball Umpire

- Expect the unexpected. You're in a totally new situation, and you can't anticipate everything.

- Pace yourself.

- Get and stay organized.

- Set up your voice mail, e-mail, and other forms of communication to establish yourself.

- Ask co-workers about their jobs to help you learn the office routine.

- Watch to see how much conversation is normal, or if employees ‛ quietly without much interaction.

First Day on the Job:
Rules for Rookies

- Be prepared to accept a lunch invitation from your boss or co-workers.

- Listen more than you talk. You can learn a lot about the company, its structure, and who is who in the organization just by keeping your ears open.

- Consider taking your notebook computer with you just in case your computer isn't set up yet.

- Bring your cell phone just in case your phone isn't hooked up yet either, but you shouldn't rely on this for more than a day or two.

- Show appreciation for help and instruction offered by co-workers.

- Try to be productive, even if you don't know much to do. At least you'll show that you are interested in working.

Dressing for Success: What You See Is What You Get

Dressing for Success:
What You See Is What You Get

*B*eing appropriately dressed is important to making a good impression in the business world. Every day you get a chance to make a statement about your professionalism through your choice of clothes. Be sure your attire says you care about the job you do by keeping the following things in mind.

What NOT to Do

- Do not wear trendy or faddish clothing. Choose something more traditional.

- Do not wear tight or suggestive clothing.

- Do not wear clothes that are baggy or wrinkled.

> "Of all the things you wear, your expression is the most important."
> Janet Lane

- Do not wear athletic shoes, sandals, or contemporary styles like platform shoes.

- Do not wear noisy jewelry like bracelets that clang together.

- Do not chew gum.

- Do not forget your hair. Don't be in a time warp with your hairstyle, but don't go too trendy either.

- Do not adjust your hairstyle or play with it in public.

> "Clothes are never a frivolity: they always mean something."
> James Laver

- Do not use heavy fragrances. Besides the fact that they may be distasteful to others around you, some co-workers may even be allergic to them.

• Do not overstuff your purse or briefcase.

What to Do

• Dress for the task at hand. If you work on a construction site, jeans are fine. But in an office, a suit is appropriate for either gender, with long sleeved shirts or blouses.

> **"What a strange power there is in clothing."**
> Isaac Bashevis Singer

• Choose clothing according to how you want to be perceived.

• Build your wardrobe with basic, but well-chosen, pieces.

• Check your company's dress policy to see what is appropriate and adhere to it religiously.

• Notice what other people in the office are wearing if you are unsure what is acceptable.

The necktie is Croatia's contribution to the traditional business suit. Croatian soldiers wore picturesque scarves tied around their necks. When they were stationed in Paris, they influenced French men to do the same. The new style was referred to as "a la Croate," which became the French word "cravate," the precursor of our modern necktie.

Dressing for Success:
What You See Is What You Get

- Strive to look businesslike, yet stylish.

- Pay attention to details. Check for loose threads and buttons.

- Choose accessories carefully.

- Style your hair fashionably, but not flamboyantly.

- Make sure your clothing fits properly.

- Women should use makeup sparingly.

- Make sure there are no makeup stains on collars and blouses.

- Wear socks or hosiery at all times. Naked feet and/or bare legs do not present a professional image.

> "Your Business clothes are naturally attracted to staining liquids. This attraction is strongest just before an important meeting."
>
> Scott Adams, Creator of "Dilbert"
> Comic Strip

- Remove hats when indoors.

- Keep shoes polished and in good repair.

- Check your breath. Good looks won't matter if you are offensive with your personal hygiene. Many people keep a toothbrush handy in their desks.

- Bathe regularly and use deodorant.

- Keep hair and nails in good repair.

- Wear your suit jacket when making calls outside the office.

- When in doubt about what to wear, choose the more conservative item.

> "Clothes can suggest, persuade, connote, insinuate, or indeed lie, and apply subtle pressure while their wearer is speaking frankly and straightforwardly of other matters."
>
> Anne Hollander

BUSINESS CASUAL

This seemingly contradictory term has caused confusion in the business community, but it really means dressing professionally, yet looking relaxed and neat. It is not a license to be sloppy or dress inappropriately.

What NOT to Do

- Do not wear old or ill-fitting clothes; business casual does not mean sloppy.

- Do not wear shorts, flip-flops, ratty jeans, or T-shirts.

- Do not wear baggy clothing. Sweat clothes are usually not allowed at most companies.

- Do not wear see-through or immodest clothes.

- Do not wear casual clothes if you have a meeting or business lunch scheduled that day, even if it's Casual Friday.

- Do not wear tight or suggestive clothing.

- Do not dress as though you are going to the beach.

- Do not wear jeans without checking to see if they are allowed.

Dressing for Success:
What You See Is What You Get

What to Do

- Consult your company policy for specific guidelines about casual attire.

- Ties are not usually required for men on business casual days, but if in doubt, wear one. If no one else is wearing one, you can always take it off.

> **Of the number of people recently surveyed, 38.6 percent of men and 42.4 percent of the women believed that people have begun dressing too casually on casual day. And yet 90 percent of the people support business casual attire year-round.**

- Always remove your hat when indoors.

- Remember that casual clothes do not mean that casual manners are acceptable.

- Be neat, even if you are not dressed up.

- Wear clothes that fit well, even if they are casual.

- Be sure to observe good hygiene even on casual days.

> **If you interview at a company on a Friday, don't assume that employees are dressed as they normally dress. Many companies have casual day on Fridays only, so employees are dressed down from their normal attire.**

Handling the Handshake:
Get a Grip!

Handling the Handshake: Get a Grip!

A handshake is a valuable form of non-verbal communication that is common in a business setting. Because handshakes usually begin and end a business encounter, they have been called "the bookends of business." Many people form their first impression largely on the quality of an initial handshake. Knowing how to shake hands confidently is vital, yet many people are confused about how to do so correctly. Observe the following Do's and Don'ts for this simple gesture.

What NOT to Do

• Do not offer a handshake to a senior-ranking officer in your company. Wait for him or her to initiate it.

• Do not stand too close or intrude on the other person's personal space while shaking hands.

• Do not offer a limp handshake, which can be interpreted as a lack of interest or lack of confidence.

• Do not shake hands with anyone if your hands (or theirs) are not clean.

Can a poor handshake knock you out of the running for a job? A recent survey indicated that the quality of a handshake ranked higher in importance during a job interview than whether an applicant had nontraditional hair color, obvious piercing or tattoos, or other unusual features.

Handling the Handshake: Get a Grip!

- Do not try to shake hands if the other person has his or her hands full, and putting everything down would be a big inconvenience.

- Do not grip too hard.

- Do not pump up and down while hands are clasped together.

- Do not double clasp during the handshake by placing your left hand on top of the clasped hands. This may be done as a gesture of added warmth for close acquaintances, but may seem presumptuous and too personal during an initial meeting.

- Do not vary handshakes because of gender. Handshakes should be genderless.

- Do not feel that you must shake hands with a colleague each time you see him or her during a workday unless there is a specific reason.

- Do not turn your wrist sideways as you shake hands.

What to Do

- Wipe your hand quickly and discreetly before the handshake if your palms are sweaty.

"Handshake Man" is the nickname of Richard Weaver, a California man known for his ability to bypass U.S. Secret Service and shake hands with the President of the United States. He has shaken hands with every President since Jimmy Carter, several times with some. Weaver believes his handshakes pass "notes from God" to the Presidents.

Handling the Handshake:
Get a Grip!

- Be aware that holding a cold drink at a business dinner will produce a cold and wet hand, so wipe that as well before shaking hands.

- Stand during a handshake unless you are elderly or disabled.

- Make eye contact as you initiate or respond to the offer of a handshake.

- Use your right hand. If the other person does not have a right hand, or it is disabled in some way, you may use your left hand to shake his or her left hand.

Handshaking is an ancient ritual that originated when men began to present their right hand, traditionally the weapon hand, open and without a sword as a sign of peace and acceptance. During the Roman Empire, the forearm was also clasped to make certain that no weapon was hidden in the sleeve. This later evolved to include just the hand.

- If greeting a group, shake as you are introduced to each person, or begin to your right and continue counter clockwise. If introducing yourself, add something like, "Hello, I'm John" as you shake hands.

- Offer a handshake using the following steps:
    - Extend your hand perpendicular to the floor with your thumb up.
    - Connect thumb joint to thumb joint.

Handling the Handshake:
Get a Grip!

- Be firm, but not crushing, with your grip.
- State your name as you extend your hand.

• Remember to let go. Holding on too long can be awkward.

• Offer a handshake at the beginning and end of a business meeting.

> **Great Britain law specifically prohibits an employer from discriminating against someone who refuses to shake hands for religious reasons.**

Introductions:
Presenting People Politely

Introductions:
Presenting People Politely

The most important thing to remember about business introductions is that a person of higher rank or status receives the introduction of someone of lower rank or status. This is done by using the name of the higher-ranking person first. Here are some other suggestions that may make this process flow a little smoother.

What NOT to Do

• Do not use terms like Mr. or Mrs. when making business introductions unless you are introducing a person of advanced age to a much younger person.

• Do not use first names unless invited to do so.

• Do not pretend to remember someone's name if you have forgotten it. Be honest and ask the person to refresh your memory.

• Do not rely on nametags at a meeting to take the place of introductions. They may make introducing yourself easier, but you should still make an effort to say your name and acknowledge the other person's.

> **Business etiquette is based on military origins, with all its hierarchy and power, whereas social etiquette is based on chivalry, which recognizes gender differences.**

• Do not put your introductions in the form of a command. Do not say, "Mr. Smith, shake hands with Mr. Brown." Rather, say, "Mr. Smith, I am pleased to present Mr. Brown."

Introductions:
Presenting People Politely

- Do not address a business superior in a familiar way unless asked to do so.

- Do not repeat names unnecessarily. Do not say, "Mr. Jones, Mr. Brown. Mr. Brown, Mr. Jones."

- Do not forget to introduce people standing together in a group. Make sure everyone knows everyone else.

What to Do

- Know the status and rank of the people you'll be introducing. Then use the name of the higher-ranking person first. To determine rank or status, remember:

  - An older person outranks a young person.
  - Out-of-town guests outrank local guests of equal status.
  - Persons with religious titles outrank lay people.
  - Senior-level businesspeople outrank junior-level people.

- Know the first and last names of each person you are introducing.

- Make eye contact.

- Pronounce each person's name correctly.

- Offer a little about each person's job if you know it.

> **"My grandfather once told me that there are two kinds of people: those who do the work and those who take the credit. He told me to try to be in the first group; there was much less competition."**
>
> Indira Gandhi

Introductions:
Presenting People Politely

- Always stand when being introduced. Even if you aren't close enough to shake hands, at least you can stand and acknowledge the introduction.

- Repeat the name of the person you have just been introduced to as a courtesy. It also gives you a chance to memorize the name and practice pronouncing it correctly.

- Make your first comment following the introduction about the other person, not about yourself.

- When you are introduced to someone new, it is common to say, "I've heard so much about you." This may imply that you have heard good and bad. Be specific in saying, "I've heard such wonderful things about your work."

- Mention anything that the people you are introducing to each other may have in common.

- Include pertinent titles such as Doctor in your introduction.

- Be sure to mention any difference in last names among family members.

- Introduce yourself if you are omitted when others introductions are made.

Business Cards: Telling Everybody Your Business

Business Cards:
Telling Everybody Your Business

Though small in size, business cards are important extensions of you and your company. You might not think there would be specific protocol about something so small, but there are things to remember about this vital part of corporate communication.

What NOT to Do

• Do not use titles such as Mr. and Mrs. on business cards. Professional designations should follow the name, such as Mary Smith, M.D.

• Do not ask senior executives for their cards. They may be reluctant to offer one because they prefer employees of lower rank to serve as contact people. Senior officers will ask for someone's card if they want it, and in exchange, may offer one of theirs.

• Do not use cards with old information crossed out and new information handwritten in.

• Do not pass out cards randomly. Give them to specific people for specific reasons.

• Do not ask people for their business card unless you have a legitimate reason for asking.

The most disrespectful thing you can do when presented with someone else's business card is to pocket it without even looking at it. Take a moment to read the card and ask or comment about something that appears on it.

Business Cards:
Telling Everybody Your Business

- Do not pocket a business card you've just received without looking at it. Taking a moment to read it indicates interest. Make a comment about the company, the logo, or something on the card.

- Do not allow yourself to run out of cards.

- Do not pass out cards during a meal. If you are specifically asked for one, pass it as discreetly as possible.

> **Al Capone's business card reportedly claimed that he was a used furniture dealer.**

What to Do

- Be sure your card offers vital information about you and your company. This should include:
    - Company's name and logo
    - Your name and title
    - Business address
    - Phone number
    - E-mail address
    - Internet address
    - Information on the reverse side in another language if you use your card internationally

- Use large enough type to make the information on your card readable.

- Carry cards in a protective holder to prevent creasing.

- Keep your cards available. You do not want to fumble for them when you need them.

> **Businessmen receiving a card from someone should never put it in their wallet and return the wallet to their back pocket. In some cultures, this is considered an insult to the one presenting the card. Put it in the case with your own cards instead.**

• Carry a few cards with you, even on social occasions. You never know when you may need one.

• Be unobtrusive if you offer a business card in a social setting. Keep the exchange private between the two of you.

• Present your card with the type side up. When someone hands you a card, take time to make a connection between the card and the face.

• Make sure you know the customs of giving business cards when dealing with other cultures. For example, in Asian cultures, you should use two hands to give and receive cards, and you should place your counterpart's card on the tabletop during a business meeting.

> **Some professionals have their business cards printed in materials like plastic and metal, which are thought to imply that the companies they represent are solid and durable. Other unusual ideas include peel-and-stick, magnetic, and foil cards.**

- Try to receive a card graciously even when it is forced on you and you don't want it. You can always discard it later.

> For something different, how about a CD business card? These new marketing tools make high-tech presentations that fit into your wallet. Each interactive card contains a combination of digital, audio, video, and text, in addition to Web links.

Communicating Correctly:
Writing Right

Communicating Correctly: Writing Right

There are times when a business letter, instead of a quick e-mail or phone call, is appropriate. A formal letter on your company's letterhead can help to establish a new relationship, send information, and serve as a record of your communication. Make sure your letters represent your company properly by following the guidelines listed below.

What NOT to Do

- Do not abbreviate or use initials for the recipient of the letter unless you are sure he or she prefers that style. For example, do not write Wm. Brown if you are writing a letter to William Brown.

- Do not use a courtesy title such as Mr. or Ms. for the recipient if you are unsure of his or her gender. It would be better to omit the title than to use an incorrect one.

- Do not begin letters with pat phrases like "Thank you for meeting with me." Make reference to something the person said or did during your meeting. Be original.

- Do not "beat around the bush." Say what you have to say clearly and directly.

- Do not try to use "big" words to impress people. Use everyday language.

- Do not use slang words; letters require more formal, but not stiff, language.

- Do not use foul or inappropriate language in a business letter, even to emphasize your point.

- Do not use abbreviations unless you are certain your reader will understand them, or unless you establish their meanings the first time you use them.

- Do not sign your full name at the bottom of the letter if you refer to the recipient by his or her first name.

> "Or don't you like to write letters. I do because it's such a swell way to keep from working and yet feel you've done something."
>
> Ernest Hemingway

- Do not mix business with pleasure. A business card should be used only with your business letters, never with your personal correspondence.

- Do not use company letterhead for the following purposes:

    - Controversial letters, such as for a "Letters to the Editor"
    - Fund-raising for political or charitable causes
    - Personal business not related to the company

- Do not rely on your spell check program for perfect copy. It won't catch legitimate words used out of context.

What to Do

- Use quality paper and envelopes for your correspondence. Your reader will see these before he or she reads a word you've written, and first impressions count.

- Think before you write. Plan what you want to accomplish with your letter.

Communicating Correctly:
Writing Right

- Use business stationery for business use, personal stationery for personal use.

- Always date your letters to document when they were sent; write out the full name of the month, do not abbreviate it.

- Make sure you have spelled the recipient's name correctly. This may sound obvious, but many people fail to do it.

- Include appropriate titles, making sure they are correct.

- When writing the name of an organization in an inside address, always follow that organization's style for spelling, spacing, etc., of its own name. For example, Photos "R" Us should be written with the quotation marks as indicated on that company's letterhead.

- Write thank-you notes by hand, not in the format of a formal business letter.

- Know who your reader will be and provide information that he or she will need.

- Be specific. Get to the point and say what you have to say.

- Choose the correct words. Do not confuse similar words such as affect and effect, it's and its.

Get and use a good stylebook for establishing your own format for letters. It will show you acceptable styles such as block, modified block, and others from which you can choose and use thereafter. It can also help with particular questions of style that you may encounter.

Is proper punctuation important to good writing? Timothy Dexter, a prominent eighteenth century New Englander, wrote his book, <u>A Pickle for the Knowing Ones</u>, without a single punctuation mark. Readers demanded that appropriate marks be added to the second edition. Dexter obliged, but with one catch: he added a page containing nothing but punctuation marks, along with a short message for readers to "pepper and salt it as they please."

- Use active voice instead of passive.

- Use down-to-earth language. Don't try to use big words to impress people.

- Use proper grammar. For example, do not use "like" when you mean "as though."

- Use humor sparingly, if at all, and only when the writer is absolutely certain it will be understood as it was intended.

- Mark sensitive, personal, or confidential letters appropriately. If you receive such a letter, it is good to let the writer know that their request for confidentiality was honored.

- Offer facts to support the information you are sending.

- Assume that other people besides your intended recipient may read what you've written. Write only what you do not mind sharing with others.

Communicating Correctly: Writing Right

- Respond to questions asked in previous correspondence in the same order as they were asked.

- When writing to outline a problem:

  - Explain your case simply and clearly to the appropriate person.
  - Indicate a time by which you hope the matter will be resolved.
  - Offer information that you anticipate will be helpful or necessary.

- When receiving a complaint:

  - Be polite and courteous in your response, even if you are unable to comply with requests.
  - Inform all colleagues who may be affected or who may offer assistance.
  - Stick to the facts and do not make judgments based on emotion.

- Sign your letters personally. An assistant may sign on your behalf if necessary.

> **Don't write everything you think! In 1989, Bryant Gumbel wrote an internal memo critical of co-workers Gene Shalit and Willard Scott. It was intended only for the eyes of the executive producer of the Today Show, but it was leaked to the public and created a firestorm of ill will toward Gumbel and negative publicity for the show.**

Communicating Correctly:
Writing Right

- Make your writing perfect—check for typos and errors in numbers and dates.

- Proofread and proofread again before sending out any type of written communication.

- Respond to letters you receive within five working days.

> **"What a lot we lost when we stopped writing letters. You can't reread a phone call."**
>
> Liz Carpenter

E-mail Etiquette:
Cyberspace Courtesy

E-mail Etiquette:
Cyberspace Courtesy

E-mail has always been used as an informal means for communication, but now it is quickly becoming the standard way to send information. Make sure your e-mails are effective communicators by observing the guidelines below.

What NOT to Do

• Do not keep old subject lines on replies that have nothing to do with the current subject.

• Do not lump several e-mails on different topics under one subject. Send separate e-mails.

• Do not use all caps; this is the equivalent of shouting in a conversation. Besides, if you use all caps for the entire text, you can't use them for emphasis.

> **About 27 percent of larger firms in the U.S. have started checking employee e-mails for obscene language or images that might constitute grounds for sexual-harassment suits.**

• Do not send anything in an e-mail that would be embarrassing if sent to others besides the intended recipient. Remember that once you send the e-mail, you have no control over where else and to whom it may be sent.

• Do not send e-mails while you are angry; personal e-mails sent in anger can be difficult to overcome, and those sent to colleagues are even worse.

• Do not respond in kind if you receive an e-mail that was obviously sent when the writer was upset.

E-mail Etiquette:
Cyberspace Courtesy

- Do not use e-mails to deliver bad news. A phone call or face-to-face meeting will allow you to deliver the news more kindly and deal with the response directly.

- Do not send last-minute changes of plans by e-mail; the intended recipient may not check his or her e-mail, and then may not know of the changes.

- Do not make your initial contact with someone by e-mail.

- Do not attach a graphic copy of your business card at the end of your e-mails.

> The @ symbol is commonly thought to be derived from the Latin preposition "ad" (at). It was first used for sending e-mail in 1971 by programmer Raymond Tomlinson, long-time employee of BBN Technologies, and is now an integral component of e-mail addresses.

- Do not share a password in an e-mail. If you must share it with someone who needs it to open an important file, do so verbally, or with a fax.

- Do not use another person's e-mail without his or her consent.

- Do not send sensitive information or personal details in your e-mail.

- Do not send chain letter e-mails to everyone in your address book.

- Do not make people scroll through long lists of addresses before getting to the subject.

- Do not say anything in an e-mail that you wouldn't say in a letter or memo.

E-mail Etiquette:
Cyberspace Courtesy

- Do not use the Reply to All button unless there is a real need to do so.

- Do not use e-mail to communicate with someone sitting near you unless you are sending it to document or recap action taken.

- Do not substitute e-mail for other forms of communication. If you go back and forth several times on the same topic, it's time to talk to the other party in person or at least by telephone.

> **"Excellence is not a skill. It is an attitude."**
> Ralph Marston

- Do not try to be funny in an e-mail unless you are absolutely certain your reader will understand correctly.

- Do not send off-color jokes or offensive language via e-mail.

- Do not discuss personal or interoffice complaints or problems in e-mail.

- Do not feel obliged to open "junk" e-mail.

- Do not take chances if material is complex or technical. If there is any chance it can be misunderstood, call or talk face-to-face instead of sending an e-mail.

- Do not forward e-mails that contain sensitive information.

- Do not label an e-mail as urgent unless it really is, and don't use the urgent label so often that it is not taken seriously.

- Do not send HTML formatted e-mails with background scenes or colored texts—they can be unreadable or lock up your recipient's computer, and they can look unprofessional.

E-mail Etiquette:
Cyberspace Courtesy

What to Do

- Adhere to standard letter-writing etiquette. If you've never spoken to the person you're e-mailing, begin with "Dear Mr. So-and-So."

- Identify yourself in each e-mail. Depending on your format, your e-mail may provide your name as the sender, or it may not.

- State a subject for each e-mail you send. With all the spam and viruses around, many people wisely choose not to open e-mail without subjects.

- Let the recipient know ahead of time if you are sending an attachment, so he or she will be sure it is safe to open.

> **"In God we trust, all others we virus scan."**
> Unknown

- Keep attachments small.

- Be brief. E-mail is not meant for long pieces of correspondence. Businesspeople who get large numbers of e-mails per day will appreciate your brevity, and will be more likely to respond.

- Alert the recipient in advance if you are sending an e-mail that needs an immediate response.

- Divide your message into easily readable segments.

- Limit the number of copies you send. Carefully consider who actually needs to be copied.

- Use short, factual sentences, and keep paragraphs short.

- Use bullets to make points, but do not use sentence fragments.

E-mail Etiquette:
Cyberspace Courtesy

- Consider your words carefully. Your reader will not have the benefit of your facial expressions to understand your tone. Some users add "smiles" at the end of their text to help with this. Here are some examples, but be careful—their use is by no means universal.

  :-)   Smiley face; happy.
  :-D   Really happy.
  ;-)   Wink (light sarcasm).
  :-(Frown.
  :-| Indifference.
  :-/   Perplexed.
  :-O   Yell; I'm surprised.
  :-p   Sticking your tongue out.
  : -X My lips are sealed.
  :-(Sad.
  :'-(I'm crying.

- Abbreviations are also found in some e-mails.

  BTW   By the way.
  FYA   For your amusement.
  FYI   For your information.
  FWIW   For what it's worth.
  IMHO   In my humble opinion.
  IOW   In other words.
  NRN   No reply needed.
  OTOH   On the other hand.
  ROTFL Rolling on the floor laughing.
  TTFN   Ta Ta for now.
  TTYL   Talk to you later.

E-mail Etiquette:
Cyberspace Courtesy

- Remember that all laws governing copyright, defamation, discrimination, and other forms of written communication also apply to e-mail.

- Think before requesting a receipt. Will it make your reader think that you don't trust him or her to respond?

- Use virus protection for your own computer safety, as well as the safety of others with whom you are communicating.

- Respond to e-mails in a timely fashion, within 24 hours if possible.

- Be aware that some people prefer that you respond to their e-mail in a particular way: typed at the bottom of their e-mail (bottom posting), or typed at the top (top posting).

- Proofread before you send your e-mail. Your spelling and grammar need to be perfect to present you as the professional you are.

- Remember that e-mail has limitations: it may be quick to send, but it cannot guarantee a quick response. If the time factor is critical, call or schedule a meeting instead.

Telephone Etiquette: Phoning with Propriety

Telephone Etiquette:
Phoning with Propriety

*W*ith all the distractions and demands of an average
office, it is easy to forego proper etiquette when talking
on the telephone. Remember that a telephone conversation
deserves the same consideration and courtesies as a face-to-
face conversation by observing the following guidelines.

What NOT to Do

• Do not make calls at unreasonable hours. Just because you can
reach someone 24/7 doesn't mean you should.

• Do not eat or chew gum while you are on the phone.

• Do not say you will be brief with a call if you know you won't. Let
the other person know what they'll be getting into.

• Do not reveal too much information. If someone is calling for Bill,
and he is in the restroom, just say he is unavailable.

• Do not ask
personal questions.

• Do not shuffle
papers or make
other distracting
noises while you
are on the phone.

> **"This 'telephone' has too many
> shortcomings to be seriously
> considered as a means of
> communication. The device is
> inherently of no value to us."**
> Western Union Internal Memo, 1876

• Do not attempt
side conversations with others in your office while you are on the
phone. Give your caller the attention he or she deserves.

• Do not shout when using the telephone.

- Do not transfer a call to another person without letting the caller know that he or she is about to be transferred.

- Do not make or accept phone calls when you already have a guest in your office.

- Do not be offended if you are asked to call back or leave a message.

- Do not just hang up if you have reached a number in error. Apologize for your error and let the person who answered know why you are hanging up.

- Do not ask co-workers to lie for you on the phone.

- Do not leave serious or upsetting messages on someone else's voice mail. Leave a message for them to call you, or you may try to reach them later if you have bad news to relay.

> **In the first month of the Bell Telephone Company's existence in 1877, only six telephones were sold!**

- Do not leave an ambiguous message that you might find funny but which would be confusing to the person you have called.

- Do not try to be amusing with your outgoing voice mail message.

What to Do

- Be sure that your automated menu facilitates incoming calls instead of discouraging them.

- Answer the phone with a simple "Hello," and identify yourself.

Telephone Etiquette:
Phoning with Propriety

- Identify yourself and your company when you are the caller. Never assume that the person you are calling will recognize your voice. Let him or her know who you are before you launch into your conversation.

- Hold the receiver so that you speak fully into it.

- Lower background noise as much as possible while you are on the phone.

- Speak directly into the receiver so that you can be understood clearly.

- Be sure of the number you are dialing before you make a call to avoid disturbing someone unnecessarily.

- Show politeness and patience on your telephone calls, even with a difficult caller.

- Listen to your incoming messages and return calls as soon as possible.

- Turn your head away from the phone if you must cough or sneeze during a call.

> **"As a teenager you are in the last stage of your life when you will be happy to hear that the phone is for you."**
> Fran Lebowitz

- Learn the names of the people you talk with frequently, but do not refer to them by their first names unless you are asked to do so.

- Ask "May I tell so-and-so who's calling?" instead of the blunt "Who's calling?" This won't be an issue if the caller follows proper protocol and identifies him or herself.

Telephone Etiquette:
Phoning with Propriety

- Call at a time likely to be convenient for the recipient of the caller. This is particularly important if you are calling to another part of the country with a different time zone than yours.

- Be sure to ask if you are calling at a convenient time.

- Get to the point of your call quickly.

- Alert the caller before you put him or her on hold. If the caller expresses concern, offer assurance that you will check with him or her periodically.

- Offer updates about every thirty seconds to the caller while he or she is on hold.

- Express yourself as clearly as possible. Remember that the person you are speaking with cannot see your facial expressions and gestures to help make your meaning clear.

- Keep voice mail messages short.

- Take and leave complete messages.

- Put the phone down gently; do not slam it down.

> **Want to know how your customers are being treated when they call? Call your own company posing as someone looking for information or as a customer with a complaint.**

Telephone Etiquette:
Phoning with Propriety

- When leaving voice messages:

  - Be brief and to the point.
  - Speak clearly and slowly.
  - Include your name, phone number, and a brief message.
  - Spell your name if you've never spoken to the person before.

- Return messages promptly. If you are not able to help the caller within twenty-four hours, at least call and leave a message about when you will be available.

> **"Well-informed people know it is impossible to transmit the voice over wires. Even if it were, it would be of no practical value."**
> *Boston Post*, 1865

- Conclude your call with "Goodbye" or some other closing remark to signal the end of the conversation.

- Follow up on the conversation by providing information promised during the phone call, or by getting materials sent promptly.

- If you will be out of the office, have your outgoing phone message let callers know. Tell them when you'll be back and when they can expect to hear from you. It is also a good idea to offer an alternate contact name and number in the meantime.

- If the caller asks for someone you don't know, make an effort to locate the person.

- Make sure your voice mail system is working and receiving calls properly. An uncooperative answering system is the same as a rude person.

The first sound-proof phone booth was built in 1877 by Alexander Graham Bell's faithful assistant, Mr. Watson. The booth was made of blankets wrapped around a box, and was intended to keep Watson's landlady from listening in on his conversations.

Conference Calls:
Talking Together with Tact

Conference Calls:
Talking Together with Tact

Conference calls provide opportunities for several colleagues to talk together at the same time. But for this to be effective, certain ground rules, such as those below, should be observed.

What NOT to Do

- Do not be late. Be ready at the time agreed upon.

- Do not use a speakerphone if you are the only person in the room. Speakerphones are for group interaction.

- Do not assume that everyone will recognize your voice. Introduce everyone at the start of the conversation.

- Do not carry on side conversations with colleagues while on the phone.

- Do not shuffle papers, tap your pencil, or do other annoying behaviors during the meeting.

- Do not reward latecomers by waiting for them.

- Do not remain silent throughout the call without announcing yourself. Other participants deserve to know who is listening to the

Approximately 10,637 Herbalife distributors and customers joined together on March 25, 2004 to set a new world's record for the largest international conference call in history. The call broke the old Guinness world record set by Governor Howard Dean and 3,466 participants in September of the previous year.

meeting, and not announcing yourself is the same as eavesdropping on a meeting.

- Do not include cell phones in the call; they may cause static and affect the quality of the call.

- Do not put your phone on hold to do something else. Your hold music will play into the conference call, and make it impossible for the others to continue. If you must handle something else, use the mute feature on your phone to block out background noise.

- Do not forget about people around you who are not involved in the conversation. Shut your door or warn your cubicle neighbors before making speakerphone calls, as speaking voice volume is increased with some technology.

What to Do
- Keep in mind that time zones of the various participants may vary, and schedule the call at a convenient time for everyone.

- Test your equipment before making the scheduled call.

- Prepare for the call by collecting appropriate materials.

- Create an agenda so all participants will know what will be covered and the estimated time involved.

- Be where you said you would be when the call comes in, and be there early.

- Disable your call waiting feature during the conference call.

- Eliminate or reduce background noise.

- Set the ground rules at the beginning of the call.

Conference Calls:
Talking Together with Tact

Most publicized conference call? In 1996, Florida residents John and Alice Martin used a radio scanner to eavesdrop on a cell phone conference call made between Republican Party leaders. The couple had a tape recorder handy at the time, recorded the call, and turned the recording over to authorities because of the ethical issues the content posed. Although the Martins requested immunity for illegally intercepting the call, they were later prosecuted and fined $500.

- Treat the call as you would a formal meeting.

- Begin the call by introducing all participants.

- Speak into the phone clearly and with appropriate volume.

- Apologize and offer to let the other person speak first if you accidentally speak over someone else.

- Identify yourself before making a statement or asking a question.

- Indicate to whom you are addressing questions.

- Make your comments and questions brief.

- Be attuned to verbal cues since you do not have the benefit of facial expressions and other nonverbal communication to convey thoughts.

- Pay attention to the conversation. Do not be busy at other tasks like checking e-mails. The other participants will be able to tell that you are distracted and not adding to the discussion.

Conference Calls:
Talking Together with Tact

- Let others know if you must step away briefly from the call.

- Stick to the agenda and the time allotted for each item.

- Make sure all participants know when the call is finished.

Maxims for Meetings: Appropriate Assemblies

Many people view meetings as a burdensome necessity, but they can actually be productive encounters if a few common sense rules are followed.

What NOT to Do

• Do not send last-minute changes of plans by e-mail; the intended recipient may not check his or her e-mail, and then may not know of the changes.

• Do not be late.

• Do not just read the agenda provided—think about it.

• Do not speak when others are speaking.

• Do not accept cell phone calls or respond to a beeper during a meeting unless it is an emergency.

• Do not interrupt anyone, even when you disagree strongly.

• Do not trash other people's ideas and suggestions. Hear them out and consider them.

• Do not monopolize the discussions or question-and-answer time.

• Do not fidget or act bored.

• Do not overload attendees with unnecessary handouts and other materials.

> **"Sleep not when others speak, Sit not when others stand, Speak not when you should hold your Peace, walk not when others Stop."**
>
> George Washington, *Rules of Civility & Decent Behavior*

- Do not put purses, briefcases, or personal items on the table.

- Do not leave early. Doing so will imply that the meeting is not worth your time or attention.

- Do not interject unrelated jokes or stories that are not pertinent to the meeting.

- Do not divulge information from the meeting that was presented in confidence.

- Do not leave without knowing if and when you will meet again, and what your responsibilities are in the meantime.

> **The "Hello" badge was initially created and used to identify guests and hosts at the first meeting of the Telephone Operators Convention in September 1880 at Niagara Falls.**

What to Do

- Let someone know you are coming if you have been asked to do so. Anticipated attendance may be critical for set-up of the meeting, or for food orders.

- Know the purpose of the meeting.

- Look your best. Even though the meeting location may offer a more casual setting than the office, remember that this is work time.

- Arrive early and get settled.

- Ask about seating if designations are not obvious. You would not want to sit down and settle in only to learn later that you should be sitting elsewhere.

Maxims for Meetings:
Appropriate Assemblies

- Offer to move elsewhere if you think you may be in someone else's place.

- Come prepared. Always bring something to write on, in addition to any handouts or materials you have received ahead of time.

- If you arrive late, get settled quietly and allow someone to give you details later about what you missed. Do not try to catch up while someone else is talking.

> "A conference is a gathering of important people who singly can do nothing, but together can decide that nothing can be done."
>
> Fred Allen

- Learn how to pronounce the speaker's name correctly and get appropriate details for a correct introduction.

- Make eye contact with the other participants. Looking at people says you are focused and interested in them and what they have to say.

- Offer a firm handshake to those you meet.

- Introduce participants who may not know each other.

- Think before you speak and keep your comments brief and to the point.

- Pay attention to the names of people you meet. Don't be so focused on what you'll say next that you do not hear names you will need to remember later.

- Use first names of people only when they have given you permission.

Maxims for Meetings:
Appropriate Assemblies

- Let others know ahead of time if you are expecting an urgent call during the meeting and will need to excuse yourself to take it. In that case, put your cell phone on vibrate so its ringing will not interfere with the meeting.

- Finish refreshments as soon as possible and get rid of cups and plates. Your place at the table should be clean and ready to do business.

- Give your undivided attention to the meeting. Listen to the material presented, and to questions posed by others.

- End the meeting at the time promised.

- Stay for the entire meeting unless absolutely prevented by other business.

- Follow up on action items after the meeting.

> **"Excellence is the gradual result of always striving to do better."**
> Pat Riley

Videoconferencing: Getting Ready for Your Close-up

Videoconferencing:
Getting Ready for Your Close-up

Even though this mode of communication has not been around as long as other forms, certain courtesies have already come to be expected of those who use it. Here are some things to remember when participating in this form of meeting.

What NOT to Do

- Do not say, "Can you hear me?" Assume that everything is working fine—someone will let you know if it is not.

- Do not stand too close to the camera.

- Do not put papers or other items over microphones.

- Do not rustle papers or tap on the microphone or table.

- Do not make excessive movements. Gesture as you normally would.

> **A recent poll indicates that as much as 71 percent of workers surveyed said they had experienced rude behavior on the job.**

- Do not make distracting sounds.

- Do not interrupt other speakers.

- Do not wear clothing that will present you unfavorably. Particular things to avoid are the following:

    - Bulky or baggy clothing—makes you look larger
    - Intense colors—red bleeds on screen, white glares, and black absorbs light
    - Noisy jewelry—creates distracting sounds
    - Shimmering fabric—reflects light

Videoconferencing:
Getting Ready for Your Close-up

- Shiny jewelry—reflects light
- Stripes, checks, and dots—blur
- Tinted lenses—make the eyes appear dark

- Do not leave the room during the meeting unless absolutely necessary.

- Do not participate in side conversations when you are not speaking.

What to Do

- Prepare everyone for the meeting by sending an agenda to all participants in advance.

- Dress "solid and simple."

- Let everyone know ahead of time who will participate.

- Inform participants when the meeting will begin and end.

- Communicate objectives of the meeting to those who will be there.

- Check all systems ahead of time for clear reception.

- Recognize that even though participants are in different places, this is a "real" meeting.

- Begin and end on time.

- Test equipment ahead of time. Have a contingency plan in case something doesn't work.

- Provide good lighting so everyone can be seen. Avoid back lighting by making sure the wall behind you is darker than your clothing.

Videoconferencing:
Getting Ready for Your Close-up

- Introduce all participants and announce any new-comers to the meeting.

- Identify all sites clearly so everyone knows from which location each speaker is speaking.

- Prepare your remarks in advance.

- Identify yourself when you speak.

- Speak loudly and clearly when it is your turn.

- Allow only one speaker at a time.

- Use names to direct questions to specific people.

- Pay attention to how others will be seeing and hearing you.

- Turn off beepers and cell phones during the meeting.

- Think of the conference as a "live" meeting. Maintain eye contact with the camera and other participants.

- Remember that you are on camera even when you are not speaking.

> **"The dictionary is the only place where success comes before work."**
> Unknown

- Eliminate background noises.

- Mute your microphone when you are not speaking.

- Allow for time delays.

- Offer information specific to your location by way of pre-meeting e-mails, handouts, or announcements before the videoconference begins.

- If meals are included in your agenda, let servers know when this is expected.

- Treat all sites the same as much as possible. If you offer food at one location, offer it at all of them.

> **The Bell Telephone System pavilion at the 1965 New York World's Fair introduced a new invention, the Picturephone. People who stopped by were amazed to be able to make a call to a nearby booth, and then to see, as well as hear, people talking in return.**

Office Behavior:
Preventing Professional
Peccadilloes

Office Behavior:
Preventing Professional Peccadilloes

Nowhere is proper behavior more important than in your own office, among the people you work with every day. Co-workers often start to take each other for granted, but efforts should be made to remember proper behavior.

What NOT to Do

• Do not barge into others' work areas.

• Do not hang around or outside a colleague's office if they are on the phone, as this can be distracting. It's better to check back later.

• Do not call colleagues "Hon," "Dear," or other terms of endearment.

• Do not use the first names of your colleagues until you are asked to do so.

• Do not eavesdrop on other people's phone conversations.

• Do not interrupt other people's conversations.

• Do not open or read mail not addressed to you.

> **"Successful people begin where failures leave off. Never settle for 'just getting the job done.' Excel!"**
> Tom Hopkins

• Do not loiter. Even if you don't have anything particular to do at the moment, your presence might keep someone else from working.

• Do not gossip. You do not want to earn a reputation as the office busybody.

Office Behavior:
Preventing Professional Peccadilloes

- Do not discuss salaries or other personal business with your co-workers.

- Do not use items in common areas that belong to others, such as food items in the company kitchen.

- Do not telephone co-workers or superiors after-hours unless you have their express permission to do so.

- Do not borrow items from co-workers' desks without permission.

- Do not just drop in on colleagues without calling or making an appointment first.

- Do not exhibit gender-specific behavior. Chivalry is not appropriate for the office; open a door for a woman only if she happens to be your CEO or your client.

- Do not wear heavy perfumes and colognes; some co-workers may be allergic.

- Do not ask colleagues about personal issues such as their health, finances, or marital status unless they initiate the conversation.

In a survey of 1,500 workers, more than 90 percent of them admitted to spreading information to co-workers on everything from office romances to pay raises. Seventy-five percent of that number admitted to telling confidential information to at least two other people the same day they learned it because it was "just too juicy to keep quiet about."

Office Behavior:
Preventing Professional Peccadilloes

- Do not give workers the "silent treatment." If there is a personal problem, address it.

- Do not belittle co-workers personally or professionally.

- Do not use discriminating language.

- Do not smoke at your desk. If you smoke, use designated areas.

- Do not sleep at your desk.

- Do not slam office doors, even when conversation

A recent survey of 1,000 office workers revealed that two out of three were regularly tardy for meetings, three out of four used foul language in the office, and most took cell phone calls during meetings.

going on outside your door is disturbing. Simply shut your door, and those talking will no doubt understand why you've closed it.

- Do not act like some tasks are beneath you. Particularly when work forces are lean, companies value employees with a spirit of cooperation who pitch in even when it's not part of their job.

- Do not address your supervisor or co-workers by their first names or nicknames when introducing a client.

- Do not use company time for idle talk or extended personal phone calls.

- Do not talk on your cell phone for extended periods during working hours.

- Do not be late for appointments and do not make others late.

Office Behavior:
Preventing Professional Peccadilloes

- Do not brush your hair, apply makeup, or do other personal tasks in public.

- Do not engage in office romances. Also, be careful of extremely close friendships with co-workers.

> **"Let us realize that the privilege to work is a gift, that power to work is a blessing, that love of work is success."**
>
> David O. McKay

- Do not monopolize office equipment such as the copier or the fax machine.

- Do not leave office equipment in disrepair, hoping the next user will fix it. If you can't fix the problem, call someone who can, and leave a note to alert others to the problem in the meantime.

- Do not try to claim credit for work that you did not rightfully earn.

- Do not keep visitors waiting unnecessarily beyond their appointment times. If a delay occurs, apologize.

- Do not eat at workstations if doing so will disturb others working in adjoining cubicles or desks. If you must eat at your desk, choose "quiet" foods.

- Do not be reluctant to ask for help if you need it.

- Do not drink alcohol during work hours, or have it at a meal when you will be going back to work.

- Do not eat food or use personal supplies that others have brought to work for their own use.

- Do not hurry through jobs thinking you will impress others with your speed. Take time to do each job well.

- Do not run to your boss with every problem. Think through problems first.

- Do not take office supplies home with you for your personal use.

- Do not say negative things about your company, or about your co-workers. Be loyal.

- Do not be emotional about business decisions.

What to Do

- Greet people in your office when you enter in the morning.

- Shake hands with everyone—men and women—the same way.

- Use your full name when introducing yourself. Don't be "Tony in Accounting." Full names give you more credibility and professional identity.

- Introduce people based on rank, not on gender.

- Be on time for meetings and appointments.

> **"Life is not so short but that there is always time enough for courtesy."**
> Ralph Waldo Emerson

- Keep confidential information to yourself, whether it's about a co-worker or the company as a whole. Loyalty is a trait that will be appreciated.

- Show your colleagues the same courtesy you would to a visitor from outside your office.

- Practice good hygiene to prevent offensive body odor.

Office Behavior:
Preventing Professional Peccadilloes

- Decorate your workspace and display personal items according to company policy.

- Have a positive attitude when you come to work each day.

- Adhere to the company dress code.

- Respect boundaries. Ask permission before entering someone else's office.

- Ask before borrowing anything from another desk.

- Return borrowed items promptly and in good condition.

- Watch your language. Profanity has no place in the office.

- Return phone calls and e-mails promptly.

- Cultivate good telephone manners.

- Return telephone calls and e-mails promptly.

- Respond to correspondence in a timely manner.

- Follow-up and provide information and materials when you promise them.

- Keep your office, cubicle, or workspace orderly and attractive.

A 2002 survey of 200 businesses revealed that companies and individuals decide who they will do business with based primarily on how well they are treated as opposed to even the quality and prices of products.

Office Behavior:
Preventing Professional Peccadilloes

- Honor your promises to co-workers. If you say you'll stay and help with a project, make sure to do it.

- Do more than you are expected to do.

- Apologize when you have kept someone waiting for you.

- Give proper credit for work done.

- Remember to remove your original documents from the fax machine or photocopier.

- Offer to get coffee, snacks, or even lunch for others you are with when getting something for yourself. Include everyone present in your office, whether they are of higher or lower rank than you.

- Clean up after yourself at common eating and working areas.

- Congratulate others on promotions and professional recognitions.

- Keep everyone working on a project informed of progress.

- Acknowledge a team effort when appropriate. Take your share of the blame when things go wrong.

- Introduce your colleagues to office visitors.

- Welcome new employees and try to help make them feel at home. The same goes for temporary and part-time workers.

- Treat all co-workers with respect, no matter if they are in an entry-level or supervisory position. You may be surprised at the ability of people at all levels to help your career.

- Remember to thank people when they help you.

Office Behavior:
Preventing Professional Peccadilloes

- Accept new assignments with enthusiasm. Every job is a job worth doing well.

- Admit mistakes when you make them. Excuses will only make you appear defensive.

- Replenish supplies if you take the last of something, or let the appropriate person know to order more.

> ## "It is easier to do a job right than to explain why you didn't."
> Martin Van Buren

Dealing with Diversity: Combining Cultures with Consideration

Dealing with Diversity:
Combining Cultures with Consideration

The ability to relate well to people of all types in the workplace is a valuable and essential skill for employees. The mixture of a variety of abilities, cultures, and races in the workplace makes for an interesting combination as people try to blend their lives into a cooperative unit within the office.

What NOT to Do

- Do not belittle cultural traditions of your co-workers if they differ from yours.

- Do not pry into details of the religious beliefs of your co-workers.

> **"We have become not a melting pot but a beautiful mosaic. Different people, different beliefs, different yearnings, different hopes, different dreams."**
> Former President Jimmy Carter

- Do not participate in conversation that ridicules people of other races, cultures, and beliefs.

- Do not recruit new employees from a narrow range of people. Cast a wide net that includes people with different backgrounds and abilities.

- Do not use language that minimizes the value of other people.

- Do not make assumptions about what others can or cannot do. You may be wrong.

What to Do

- Be respectful when a colleague celebrates a religious holiday with which you are unfamiliar. Ask about the holiday and its significance.

Dealing with Diversity:
Combining Cultures with Consideration

- Choose a variety of foods at office celebrations to accommodate cultural or religious dietary restrictions.

- Choose non-religious holiday standards for music at office parties.

- Offer others the respect and courtesy you want from them.

- Treat people equally regardless of their gender.

- Be tolerant of people as they try to learn new languages and idiomatic expressions. Appreciate the effort they are making.

- Accommodate, but do not draw undue attention to, co-workers' disabilities.

- Make sure that your workplace is in compliance with the Americans with Disabilities Act.

- Establish procedures to report incidents of harassment or discrimination.

> **"The price of a democratic way of life is a growing appreciation of people's differences, not merely as tolerable, but as the essence of a rich and rewarding human experience."**
>
> Jerome Nathanson

- Take seriously any indication from an employee that he or she has been a victim of discrimination or intolerance.

- Offer diversity training for employees if possible. Many small companies cannot afford one-on-one training, but videos and online training are usually more affordable.

Dealing with Diversity:
Combining Cultures with Consideration

• Respect input from all employees, even if it differs from yours.

• Post all job openings and give everyone an equal chance to apply for them.

Resolving Conflicts: Blessed Are the Peacemakers

Resolving Conflicts:
Blessed Are the Peacemakers

Conflicts are certain to occur as people with various personalities, goals, and expectations try to work together. They are a normal part of doing business. Make sure that even small disagreements do not escalate into larger ones by dealing with them properly as they arise.

What NOT to Do

• Do not ignore signs that a conflict is brewing.

• Do not avoid the conflict, hoping it will go away. It won't. Even if it appears to have been put to rest, it may reappear in times of stress, probably at the worst possible moment.

• Do not meet separately with people in conflict. This may polarize positions further.

• Do not think that the only people affected by the conflict are the participants. Everyone in the office will feel the tension of the situation.

> **It is estimated that as much as 30 percent of managers' time may be spent in managing conflict.**

• Do not use judgmental language such as "you should" or "you must."

• Do not use "you" statements. Rather, use "I" statements.

• Do not exaggerate or make judgments about co-workers. Focus on the facts.

• Do not use extreme words like "never" and "always."

• Do not interrupt when people are explaining their positions.

What to Do

• Address the problem as soon as you are certain it will not resolve itself.

• Use your ears. Listening is the key to finding solutions.

• Get as much information as possible about the difference. Identify the key points without making accusations.

• Stay calm.

• Examine your own actions, policies, and procedures to see if they have played any part in creating the conflict.

> **"He who wishes to secure the good of others, has already secured his own."**
> Confucius

• Focus on the issues, not on personalities.

• Ask questions.

• Show understanding for all points of view.

• Pay attention to body language in meetings to discuss the problem. It may indicate which people are open and which are resistant to resolution of the problem.

• Recognize the legitimacy of each party's needs.

• Stay professional.

• Look for solutions together.

• Give each person your full attention by making eye contact.

Resolving Conflicts:
Blessed Are the Peacemakers

• Nod in understanding, and ask for clarification when needed.

• Keep communication channels open.

• Assure all parties that you have faith in their abilities to reach an amiable solution.

• Enlist an outside mediator if necessary.

• Offer seminars and classes to promote cooperation in the office.

Meals and Manners: When the Dining Room Is the Boardroom

Meals and Manners:
When the Dining Room Is the Boardroom

There is as much business conducted in the dining room as in the boardroom. This is one place where all your social skills come together: your table manners as well as your ability to interact with others courteously are on display. Make sure you handle yourself professionally by knowing the rules of etiquette for business lunches and dinners.

What NOT to Do

• Do not be late.

• Do not call the waiter or waitress "Honey" or other terms of endearment.

• Do not order anything crunchy or messy, or that you eat with your hands.

• Do not lean on the table. Sit up straight.

• Do not put your elbows on the table, but you may rest your hands there.

> **"Being Set at meat Scratch not neither Spit Cough or blow your Nose except there's a Necessity for it."**
> George Washington, *Rules of Civility & Decent Behavior*

• Do not bring your face toward the plate; bring the utensil up to you.

• Do not start eating until your host or hostess does, or until everyone has been served.

• Do not fill your mouth with too much food.

• Do not tuck your napkin into your waistband or collar.

- Do not talk with your mouth full. It will be difficult to understand what you're saying, and unpleasant to see.

- Do not play with the table utensils.

- Do not apply makeup, comb your hair, or do other grooming at the table.

- Do not talk loudly.

- Do not wear a hat at the table.

> **At an American business meal, it is considered inappropriate to get down to business before the waiter has handed you the menu. In other countries, you don't talk business until the first glass of wine has been poured and the host offers a toast.**

- Do not salt or pepper your food before tasting it.

- Do not mix or mash your food together.

- Do not be flustered by accidents such as dropping a utensil. Excuse yourself, smile, and continue the conversation. Your ability to handle a glitch with grace will offset the blunder.

- Do not blow on hot food or drink to cool it.

- Do not sip coffee from your saucer or spoon.

- Do not season any dish that serves everyone at the table. Season only your own food.

- Do not use your thumb to push food onto your fork or spoon.

- Do not help yourself to an item you have been asked to pass until the person who originally requested it has served him or herself.

Meals and Manners:
When the Dining Room Is the Boardroom

- Do not panic if you spill something. Be calm, apologize, and allow your server to help with cleanup.

- Do not smoke at the table.

- Do not slurp soup or coffee.

- Do not eat the garnish.

- Do not lift your soup bowl to drink the final drops. Tilt the bowl away from you and scoop what you can with the spoon pushing way from you. Do not try to get every bit.

- Do not leave a spoon in your coffee or tea.

- Do not lick your fingers. Use your napkin to wipe your hands.

- Do not pick up dishes and hold them in your hand while you eat.

- Do not butter an entire slice of bread at once. Break the bread or roll into bite-sized pieces and butter each piece as you need it.

> **The first plates were made of large rectangular pieces of bread and were called "trenchers." Bread also often served as one's napkin and hot pad.**

- Do not gobble your food. Pace yourself so that you finish about the same time as everyone else.

- Do not bring up politics, religion, or other controversial topics during the meal. Neutral topics are sports, common acquaintances, and common interests.

- Do not answer your cell phone during the meal. It should be turned off anyway.

- Do not leave the table during the meal except in an emergency. In that case, simply excuse yourself and leave.

- Do not remove food particles from your teeth at the table. If you cannot wait until the end of the meal, excuse yourself and go to the restroom to correct the problem.

- Do not order alcoholic beverages. Even if others are doing so, there is always the chance that drinking too much will allow undesirable behavior.

> **"Bad table manners, my dear Gigi, have broken up more households than infidelity."**
> Isabel Jeans to Leslie Caron in the movie *Gigi*, 1958

- Do not push your dishes away to signal that you are finished eating. Placing your utensils in the four o'clock position indicates that your plate may be cleared.

- Do not ask for a doggy bag.

- Do not try to help servers by handing them plates or holding glasses for them to fill.

What to Do

- Put briefcases, purses, and other personal items on the floor, not on the table.

- Be courteous to the wait staff. Ask politely for anything you may need.

Meals and Manners:
When the Dining Room Is the Boardroom

- Consider left-handedness and right-handedness of guests when you are being seated.

- Turn off your cell phone, beeper, and anything else that might interrupt your meal.

- Place your napkin in your lap right away when you sit down. Do not snap it open; just put it on your lap.

- Order with care. Stick with dishes that can be managed easily and are not messy.

- Chew with your mouth closed.

- Know how to use a standard table setting. Start with utensils on the outside and work your way "in." You will normally find the following:

> **In medieval times, utensils were wrapped in napkins to keeps others from putting poison on them.**

Salad fork – If a salad is served before the entrée, this smaller fork will be found to the left of the dinner fork. If salad is to be served after the entrée, as in some very formal meals, the salad fork will be to the right of the dinner fork.

Dinner fork – This is the largest fork; it is used to eat the entrée as well as side dishes.

Soup spoon/fruit spoon – If soup or fruit is served as a first course, this spoon is the outer-most utensil on the right side of the plate.

Dinner knife – This large knife is used for the entrée, and is found just to the right of the plate.

Butter knife – This small knife is placed across the edge of the bread plate. It is placed there each time after it is used to butter the bread.

Dessert fork/dessert spoon – These might be paired and placed above the dinner plate before the meal, or they might be brought to you with dessert.

- Watch what others do if you are unsure about what utensil to use.

- Cut food by holding it with a fork as you cut it with a knife.

- Order carefully. It is better to stick with foods that are eaten with a fork and knife. But there are some foods that may be properly eaten with your fingers, such as these listed below:

  Artichoke – The artichoke is the leaf-enclosed flower bud of a plant in the thistle family. It is usually served steamed with a dipping sauce. To eat it, pull a leaf off, dip it, scrape the flesh from the base of the leaf with your top teeth, and discard the leaf on the plate provided for that purpose. Continue eating the leaves until the prickly "choke" is revealed. Switch to fork and knife, first to remove the choke, then to eat the heart and base.

  Asparagus – Asparagus may be eaten with the fingers if it is not covered with sauce, or is not too mushy to pick up easily. Of course you may use a fork and knife if you prefer.

  Bacon – Bacon may be eaten with the fingers for a very practical reason: if you tried to cut it with a fork, it would probably shatter, and the pieces would then be nearly impossible to "round up" with your fork.

Bread – Bread should always be broken, never cut with a knife. Tear off a piece no bigger than two bites and eat that before tearing off more. If butter is provided, butter the small piece just before eating it. Some experts advise putting a small amount of butter on your own plate before putting it on the bread. If you need more butter, get it from your own plate instead of going back to the common source where others are getting theirs.

Cherry Tomatoes – Except when served in a salad or other dish, cherry tomatoes are eaten with the fingers. Remember that they squirt, so find one small enough to eat whole.

Cookies – Unless cookies are broken into small pieces in your dessert, in which case you would eat them with a spoon, they are eaten with your fingers.

Chips, French Fries, Fried Chicken, and Hamburgers – These items won't be served at a formal dinner, but when you are served them, eat them with your fingers unless they are so messy that they absolutely require a knife and fork.

Fruits and Berries on the Stem – Fruits on their stems are intended to be eaten with the fingers. When they are served in a bowl without stems, use a spoon.

Hors d'oeuvres, Canapés, Crudités – Almost everything served at a cocktail party or during a pre-meal hour is intended to be eaten with the fingers. Even when these are served at a regular meal, they may be eaten with the fingers.

Pizza – Pizza is cut into manageable pieces and then picked up and eaten with the fingers.

Sandwiches – Unless they are open-faced, too tall to fit in the mouth, or saturated with sauces or mushy fillings, sandwiches should be eaten with the fingers.

- Use utensils if there is any doubt about how a particular food should be eaten.

- Cut meat one piece at a time, not all at once.

- Rest silverware on your plate when speaking.

> In the sixteenth and seventeenth centuries, having one's own toothpick was very popular. They were made of gold or silver, and were often pinned to their owner's clothes.

- Ask your server for a clean piece of silverware if yours is dirty.

- Discreetly alert your server if your food is not thoroughly cooked or if there is a foreign object in your food. He or she will see that the problem is taken care of.

- Reach for and pass items to others only if you are the one closest to the items.

- Maintain eye contact with others throughout the meal.

- Limit or forego alcohol consumption. It is easy to underestimate how much you have had as conversation and the meal progresses.

- Ask for items that you cannot easily reach. Do not reach across others to get dishes.

Meals and Manners:
When the Dining Room Is the Boardroom

- Excuse yourself by saying "Excuse me" to no one in particular if you happen to burp or hiccup during the meal.

- Use a tissue, not your napkin, when a sneeze is imminent.

- Insist that other diners go ahead and eat if your plate is the only one late in being served.

- Pass the salt and pepper together when asked to pass either.

- Pace your eating so that you finish about the same time as everyone else.

- Take small, manageable bites.

- Remove tough gristle or a bad piece of food from your mouth using the same utensil it went in with. Place the food on the edge of your plate, covered with some other food.

- Indicate that you have finished eating by placing your knife and fork parallel to each other, diagonal from bottom right to top left on the plate.

- Indicate that you have not finished by crossing your fork and knife like an X over your plate.

> **There is a European superstition that a diner who leaves the napkin on his or her chair will never sit at that table again.**

- Place your napkin to the left of your plate on the table when you are finished, but never until everyone is finished eating and drinking. If your plate has already been cleared, place your napkin where the plate had been.

Meals and Manners:
When the Dining Room Is the Boardroom

• Wait until the meal is finished before initiating serious talk of business.

• Thank your host or hostess for the meal before you leave.

Gift-giving:
Proper Protocol for Presents

Gift giving is an excellent way to maintain business relations. But don't let your good intentions be ruined by an inappropriate or offensive gift. Note the following before deciding on a gift for your favorite employee or client.

What NOT to Do

- Do not give elaborate gifts that could be misinterpreted as bribery. It is important that the recipient not be made to feel uncomfortable by the gesture.

- Do not give gifts to associates with whom you are negotiating a deal.

- Do not give personal gifts bearing a company logo. Logos belong on such common novelties as mugs and key chains.

- Do not give food items as gifts unless you know for sure the recipient is not prohibited from eating the items due to health or religious restrictions.

- Do not assume that a gift will strengthen a distant relationship with a client.

When logo gifts are used on a rare occasion, the gift must be of the highest quality and good taste, and the logo must be small so that it does not look as though the gift is really a corporate advertisement, or that you are using the opportunity to "dump" promotional items.

- Do not give gifts that are personal enough to touch the skin, such as perfume or jewelry.

- Do not give gifts of alcohol unless you know the attitude of the recipient toward it.

- Do not send anonymous gifts. With heightened security in so many areas of our lives, no one wants to accept a gift from an unknown giver.

> "The manner of giving is worth more than the gift."
>
> Pierre Corneille

- Do not give items tied to a religious holiday.

- Do not overlook packaging. Unique wrapping can make even a modest gift special.

- Do not enclose your business card as the only gift card. If you enclose your card, you may slash through your printed name and add a more informal signature, and any personal note you wish to include.

- Do not give humorous gifts that may be misunderstood.

- Do not give even gag gifts that may be perceived as offensive because of sexual or cultural connotations.

What to Do

- Check your company policy on gift giving before you do anything. See what is permissible, and whether there are restrictions on the value of the gift as well.

- Pay attention to the recipient's tastes. Try to choose gifts fitting to his or her hobbies or interests, not yours.

Gift-giving:
Proper Protocol for Presents

- Make sure your gift does not clash with religious or cultural laws of the recipient.

- Choose a gift that does not have an unintended meaning. For example, if sending flowers, send an arrangement or a potted plant instead of roses, which traditionally have romantic overtones.

- Consider sending a group gift if you have contact with many people in a particular company.

- Deliver the gift personally or at least have a messenger take it when possible. When this is not practical, at least make certain that gifts are accompanied by a brief, personalized, handwritten note.

> **Practical items for the office make good gifts. Some examples are a business card holder, an attractive pen, or a hardbound thesaurus or dictionary.**

- Be aware of particular international rules that apply when giving gifts to those outside the United States.

- Consider giving a donation to a favorite charity of the recipient.

- Give gifts in a timely manner. For example, if you're giving a birthday gift, make sure to give it on or before the birthday.

- Be careful when giving gifts to a superior, which could be misinterpreted as a bribe, or at the very least, trying to ingratiate yourself with your boss. Having everyone in the department get together for a group gift is a much better idea.

- Resist giving even group gifts for every little thing. Legitimate occasions include:

  - Death in an employee's immediate family
  - Illness of an employee
  - New baby in an employee's family
  - Retirement of an employee
  - Wedding of an employee

- Present the gift well by wrapping it beautifully.

- Be thoughtful about what you write on an enclosed card.

- Send a note to graciously decline a gift that is inappropriate or exceeds the standards allowed by company policy.

Imagine shopping 'til you drop and getting paid for it! Some companies employ corporate gift buyers to handle the large volume of gift giving that is a major part of their public relations plan.

International Interactions: Guidelines for Going Global

*W*hether you are going to live and work in a foreign country, or just deal with foreign countries occasionally, there are things you need to know about working internationally. Different cultures have different customs. Disrespect toward any aspect of life in another country may undo a business deal that took months to develop. The more knowledgeable you are about any foreign country, the less likely you will be to offend someone in that country.

What NOT to Do

• Do not criticize national politics of the other country.

• Do not give gifts without knowing their cultural implications.

• Do not let fear of making a blunder make you appear to be stiff or unfriendly. If you make a mistake, acknowledge it, apologize, and move on.

• Do not use idiomatic expressions that may not translate well in conversations. Examples are "Take the bull by the horns," and "Run-of-the-mill."

> **"Be ready or be lost; if you don't think globally, you deserve to be unemployed and you will be."**
>
> Peter Drucker, *Business Week*

• Do not make gestures, even those that are harmless in the United States: they may have meanings in other countries that are quite different from your intention. For example, the "OK" sign (with index finger and thumb together, and other fingers extended) is considered obscene in some cultures.

- Do not be overly familiar by calling a colleague by his or her first name until you are asked to do so.

- Do not assume that genders are treated the same in other countries. For example, in Bangladesh, Muslim women eat separately from men.

> **In Italy, flicking one's ear signifies that a nearby gentleman is effeminate.**

- Do not take sides, however good-natured, on local rivalries. For example, Belgians will often tell jokes about the Dutch and vice versa. Leave the partisan comments to them.

- Do not refuse hospitality. Declining food or drink might be mistaken as a sign of mistrust on your part.

What to Do

- Acquire as much knowledge of the native language as possible. At least be able to ask and answer simple, everyday questions.

- Learn the proper name of the country and how citizens refer to it. For example, the Soviets call their country the Soviet Union, not Russia.

> **Never give a gift of a clock to a Chinese associate, to whom clocks are a symbol of death.**

International Interactions: Guidelines for Going Global

- Know basic information about the country, such as its form of government and its head of state. Other information that may be helpful to know would include:

    - Leading exports
    - National religion
    - National holidays
    - Native celebrities
    - Pressing international issues

- Here are some places where you can find the information you need:

    - Colleagues who work there
    - Commerce Department in Washington, DC
    - Consulate of the country
    - First-hand accounts from people who have visited the country
    - Library
    - National tourist agencies
    - State Department

- Become familiar with the typical business dress for the country.

- Familiarize yourself with religious taboos.

- Learn the metric system if used in the country where you'll be working.

- Do your research.

- Be careful of using even common words that may have a different meaning outside the U.S. For example, if you don't actually want to "bathe," don't ask for the "bathroom." If you don't want to "rest," don't ask for the "restroom." Learn and use terminology correct for the particular company you are working with.

- Take advantage of every opportunity to learn something new about the country with which you are dealing.

- Offer your business card with your information printed in English on one side and in the country's language on the other side.

- Watch out for body language that might be misinterpreted.

- Be sure to greet colleagues appropriately according to their local protocol.

- Schedule meetings and appointments at a time typical for a particular country. For instance, do not schedule a breakfast meeting in a country that prefers business to be conducted later in the day.

- Learn the particulars about how a given country deals with business issues: Do meetings start on time or later than scheduled? How far in advance must you schedule an appointment?

- Know local attitudes toward religious practices and how they apply to everyday life, such as what foods must be avoided, and what days are sacred.

- Be aware of gender roles in foreign countries: how each gender is regarded, what is expected of each, and what is proper for each. This may even affect after-hours behavior in a foreign country. For example, in some countries it is not proper for a woman to eat or drink alone in a restaurant. Even if she is doing nothing wrong, she may suffer in prestige because of local interpretation of her behavior.

International Interactions:
Guidelines for Going Global

- If you must speak through an interpreter, look at the person doing the speaking (or with whom you are speaking), not at the interpreter. The interpreter is only a representative of your colleague.

- Be careful of how you conduct yourself even in your leisure time. You never know who might be watching you.

Asking for a Raise:
Going for the Gold

Asking for a Raise:
Going for the Gold

*A*sking for a raise is never easy, but if you prepare *properly, it won't be the white-knuckle experience you fear. These hints can help you prepare for the dreaded conversation and increase your chance of success.*

What NOT to Do

- Do not assume that just because you're good at your job, raises will automatically come to you.

- Do not be reluctant to ask for a raise if you can show good reasons why you deserve it.

- Do not ask for a raise on a whim. Consider your request carefully before you present it.

- Do not be intimidated by the process of asking for a raise. Ask if you think you have earned it.

- Do not think you will get a raise just because you are dependable and your attendance is good. Those things may be increasingly hard to find, but they are still expected.

> **Timing is everything! The best time to ask for a raise is when you have successfully finished a project in the office, or even a personal one like a work-related degree, that makes you more valuable to the company.**

- Do not expect a raise just because you've got a big workload. Work volume is not a legitimate reason to ask.

- Do not go behind your immediate superior to his or her boss to ask for a raise.

- Do not bring up the subject of salary with your boss in front of other people.

- Do not blindside your boss by catching him or her in the break room to ask for a raise. Make an appointment to allow time for a proper discussion.

- Do not schedule your discussion with your boss before an important presentation or when he or she is tired from a business trip.

- Do not be emotional during the conversation.

- Do not appear to be desperate.

- Do not use the word "raise." Talk about your performance and your compensation.

- Do not focus on the increase you need. Your boss won't care that you have a new car

> **Experts suggest that you not schedule your salary discussion on a Monday morning or a Friday afternoon, which are busy times for most people and may not allow the time you need.**

to pay for or that your mortgage payment just went up. Offer professional, not personal, reasons why you deserve the increase.

- Do not expect a raise because someone in a similar job got one. Today's workers wear many hats, and jobs may be quite different even though the titles are similar.

Asking for a Raise: Going for the Gold

- Do not tell your boss that you heard co-workers have received higher raises, even if it's true. Talking about someone else's situation is a turn-off. All that matters is yours.

- Do not threaten to leave if you don't get the raise. That makes you an adversary.

- Do not tell your boss you have another job offer unless you really do. He or she may call your bluff.

- Do not overlook non-monetary benefits that you may already be receiving. If your company offers a schedule that accommodates a particular need, or the chance to learn new skills on the job, those should be considered.

- Do not give up if your request is denied. Be willing to revisit the topic later.

- Do not do anything without thinking it over carefully if your request is denied.

What to Do
- Approach this matter in a professional and well thought-out manner.

- Check company policies about raises. Read your employee handbook if you have one.

Statistics show that it is less expensive and less disruptive to an employer to keep a current employee at a higher salary than to recruit and train a new employee.

Asking for a Raise:
Going for the Gold

- Do your homework. Check what the market is paying for your skills and abilities. There are web sites that offer this information.

- Consider the particulars of your situation. Are you a seasoned veteran, a part-time employee, or a new hire? A part-time worker, for example, might not be eligible for a raise until he or she is full-time. Relatively new workers might have to fulfill a probation period before pay is increased.

- Increase your visibility before you ask. Volunteer for projects or committees outside your normal area of responsibility.

- Have a plan and a strategy before meeting with your supervisor.

- Find the right time to ask. Timing really is everything. Aim for a time when your boss isn't overwhelmed or pressured. Ask when you have just done something great and the boss knows it.

- Notice how well your company/department is doing. If things are not going well, now is not the time to ask.

- Find the right place. Discussions this important should be held in private, not during a chance meeting in the elevator.

- Prepare an accomplishment log. Make a list of what you've done. Regardless of your profession, you can always show how you contributed to the bottom line of the company.

> **Give specific examples of your contributions when asking for a raise. For instance, if you are a sales representative, list the dollar amount of sales you generated this year compared to last year.**

Asking for a Raise:
Going for the Gold

- Be specific with the information you offer. Include percentages, facts, and figures.

- Ask someone you trust (not a colleague) to review your list to see if there are gaps that should be filled in.

- Provide a copy of your accomplishments in writing so your boss can review them later.

- Offer copies of past evaluations and positive e-mails or memos from supervisors or co-workers about your performance.

- Be willing to accept more responsibility for higher wages.

- Keep the conversation confidential. There are few topics more personal than salary. Don't talk loosely about yours.

- Be confident. Project a positive self-image.

- Have a goal in mind but be realistic. Know the parameters that are possible.

- Ask for an amount higher than you will actually accept to allow for negotiation.

- Be flexible in considering other perks that might be offered such as extra vacation time or tuition reimbursement.

- Use "I" wording: "I've done ...." "You" language will sound accusatory.

- Be prepared with an answer in case your boss asks what you will do if you don't get the raise.

- Allow your boss time to think it over.

Asking for a Raise:
Going for the Gold

- Be persistent if your boss doesn't follow up on your discussion.

- Ask (respectfully) for an explanation if you are turned down.

- Take time to consider all your options objectively and calmly if you are turned down.

- Request a reevaluation in six months if you are refused a raise because of particulars like poor attendance. Ask if your boss will reconsider once you've improved in the deficient areas.

The Rabble-A Players Comedy Troupe, a group of mostly community college professors, addresses disappointing wages and benefits with their performance of "The Twelve Days of Bargaining." Lyrics by Linda Janakos list things offered instead of pay increases, including lottery tickets, workshops, pats on the back, and extra pencils.

Hiring and Firing:
Holding and Folding 'Em

Hiring and Firing:
Holding and Folding 'Em

Employees are the most important assets a company has. They must be carefully chosen and encouraged to work at maximum potential. But even under the best of circumstances, there will be times when workers must be terminated. Learn how to handle both ends of this spectrum by reviewing the guidelines provided below.

HIRING

What Not to Do

• Do not ask for unnecessary qualifications. For example, unless the position you are filling requires a college degree, do not ask for one.

• Do not ask illegal questions when you interview. Off-limit questions include, but may not be limited to, those related to:

> "When you hire people that are smarter than you are, you prove you are smarter than they are."
>
> R.H. Grant

- Age
- Birthplace
- Disability
- Health status
- Marital/family status
- National origin
- Race
- Religion
- Sexual orientation

• Do not consider hiring family members or friends unless you are absolutely sure your personal relationship with them will not be affected by your working together.

- Do not ask questions or make comments not related to the job. Focus on the job to be filled and how the applicant may be suited for it.

- Do not do too much of the talking during the interview. Allowing the applicant to talk will help you make a more informed decision about him or her.

- Do not rush with your questions. Be sure the job candidate has finished with each answer before starting another.

What to Do

- Adhere to relevant state and federal hiring rules.

- Think before you hire a new employee. Evaluate your company's needs, define the job you want to fill, and decide what kind of employee can best fill that position.

- Make a detailed list of the tasks you will want the new employee to perform.

Government statistics show that a full 30 percent of all business failures result from poor hiring techniques.

- Decide on minimum educational and experience requirements and be direct in communicating those to people you interview.

- Define the salary range by finding out what other companies in your area are paying people in similar positions.

- Consider if and how you will want the position to grow and change over the next several years.

Hiring and Firing: Holding and Folding 'Em

- Divide your qualifications into those the new employee must have and those he or she should have.

- Develop a recruiting plan to identify the best sources for qualified people.

- Be sure to check with all laws that pertain to hiring and make sure you are in compliance.

- Set a target date by which you will have someone hired.

- Publicize the opening in ways that would be the most likely to identify the best employee for the job. If it is an entry-level position, for example, you might want to advertise on a college campus.

- Decide who will receive applicant calls. All pertinent calls should be forwarded to that person.

- Evaluate resumes and make an initial screening. Red flags to indicate those to eliminate would include gaps in employment record, a pattern of short tenures in other positions, and non-relevant experience or education.

The U.S. Department of Labor reports that the average "bad hire" that leaves a company within six months costs the company approximately $40,000 in severance pay, training, wasted human resource time, possible search firm fees, loss of productivity, and impact on employee morale.

Hiring and Firing:
Holding and Folding 'Em

- A brief pre-interview phone call can help you save time by eliminating unqualified applicants up front. You can discover obvious disqualifying facts during a brief conversation.

- Interview qualified candidates in a quiet place where you will not be disturbed.

- Have everyone who will work with the new employee interview him or her. This is especially important for a small office, where a good mix of personalities is important.

- Arrange the seating in a relaxed way to promote conversation.

- Make a list of questions you want to ask during the interview.

- Look beyond the resume, which won't show attitudes and values.

- Document disqualifying responses from applications not chosen. This can serve as back-up in case there are questions about why someone was not hired, and may also be useful if you review the current applications for a later position.

- Let other employees know once a decision has been made to add another employee.

- Notify those not selected that you have filled the position.

- Decide who will show the new employee around the office on the first day.

- Have a work area prepared on the first day the new employee begins. He or she will feel at loose ends if a place is not ready the first day.

- Introduce new employees to everyone in the company, and provide information about the company.

- Invite the new employee to have lunch with other workers as he or she learns the office routine.

FIRING

What Not to Do

- Do not fire anyone on the spur of the moment. Take time to plan how you will let the employee go and to gather documentation you will need to reinforce your decision.

- Do not prolong what has to be done. If terminating an employee is inevitable, take care of it as soon as is feasible.

- Do not fabricate reasons for the termination. Do not say that downsizing is to blame if the problem is really a performance issue.

- Do not be surprised if the employee doesn't understand the details as you explain them. This is an emotional event, and it may be too much to absorb at once.

> **CBS offers a new twist to getting fired with its new reality show, <u>Fire Me, Please</u>. Two people start new jobs on the same day and try to get their unsuspecting bosses to fire them. The contestant who gets fired closest to the 3:00 p.m. deadline without going past it wins the $25,000 prize.**

Hiring and Firing:
Holding and Folding 'Em

- Do not fire someone at an inappropriate time, such as right before a holiday, or just after he or she has lost a family member.

- Do not let the employee know he or she is being let go where others may overhear your conversation. Offer the courtesy of complete privacy for this important conversation.

- Do not share reasons for or details of the termination with other employees. A breach of confidentiality could pave the way for a lawsuit.

What to Do

- Choose the best time. Some people think Friday afternoons are best, some think earlier in the week.

- Back up the employee's computer files before you break the news just in case he or she tries to delete or remove files.

- Call the employee aside and say something like, "I have something to discuss with you."

- Have a human resources representative present as a witness to make sure the meeting follows HR policies, and to answer questions about severance and benefits.

- Consider using a neutral site for the discussion. The terminated employee may want to prolong the meeting, or go over details of the termination which the boss will not have to stay for. At a neutral site, the boss is free to leave at any time.

- Explain that he or she is being let go.

- Get to the point quickly.

Hiring and Firing:
Holding and Folding 'Em

- Summarize the main reasons for the firing, recap warnings that may have been given, and missed opportunities to improve his or her performance.

- Have the reason(s) in writing and ask the employee to sign the document to indicate that these items have been explained to him or her.

- Be prepared to take responsibility for the decision if you are asked whose decision it was.

- Show appropriate concern for the impact that being fired will have to the employee.

> **Billy Martin was fired five times from his job as manager of the New York Yankees by owner George Steinbrenner.**

- Recognize that you may also have an emotional reaction to the process even if it is a necessary decision for the good of the company.

- Answer any questions the terminated employee may have.

- Extend reasonable courtesies as he or she leaves. Give him or her the opportunity to say goodbye to co-workers.

- Offer any assistance you have available for finding a new job or for getting counseling if needed.

- Have a final paycheck ready to give the terminated employee.

- Make sure company property such as laptops and keys to vehicles are turned in.

- Be prepared to have the employee escorted out if he or she makes a scene, or threatens you or other employees.

- Document the meeting by putting details of the meeting in writing and filing a copy with human resources.

> "Getting the sack" is a slang term that means "getting fired." It came from a time when mechanics traveling in search of work carried their tools in a sack or bag. When they were discharged, their sacks were returned to them so they could take their tools and look for a job elsewhere.

Leaving Your Job:
Deportment for Departing

IF YOU ARE FIRED

Getting fired is something everyone hopes will never happen to them, but the reality is that it happens to the best of us, and for a variety of reasons. If this happens to you, handle it with grace and make the most of it by following the items on the lists below.

What NOT to Do

• Do not beat yourself up over being fired. It happens to many people every day, so you are not alone.

• Do not see yourself as a failure because of the firing. There are many variables when anyone is let go from a job, and other factors may be the primary cause.

• Do not wallow in the experience. Grieve for your loss, and then get on with your life.

• Do not assume a negative attitude. Yes, this is a difficult experience, but you can get through it. Others have.

• Do not be angry. Control your emotions as you prepare to leave the company.

Sometimes, it's for the best! Harry Potter creator J.K. Rowling lost her job as a secretary because she was caught writing stories on her computer. She used her severance pay to begin the first Harry Potter book, and she is a billionaire today thanks to her work as a writer.

Leaving Your Job:
Deportment for Departing

- Do not sign any papers related to your termination unless you are sure of their content.

- Do not hesitate to negotiate a good severance package for yourself. Items for discussion include:

  - Amount of final salary
  - Assistance in relocating
  - Counseling support
  - Extension of benefits
  - Terms of final salary

- Do not lie about what happened when you are asked by prospective employers. It will come back to haunt you.

- Do not talk poorly about your former boss or employer as you search for a new job. It can, and will, catch up with you.

- Do not burn bridges. Maintain a cordial relationship between you and your boss, as well as with your co-workers. You may need a reference during your job hunt and you never know where that will come from.

> **New York Mayor Michael Bloomberg was handed his pink slip and $10 million when the company he worked for was sold in 1981. This allowed him, at thirty-nine years of age, to go on to create a billion-dollar media empire.**

- Do not take anything with you that belongs to the company, not even small desk accessories.

Leaving Your Job:
Deportment for Departing

- Do not punish yourself for this experience. Pamper yourself by making time for things you enjoy.

- Do not let go of your dreams. Being terminated may offer you a chance to pursue something you have always wanted to try.

What to Do
- Find out the reasons behind being let go. Ask specifically if something personal about your work is to blame, or if the company is simply downsizing.

- Assess how many unused vacation/personal days you have and see if you will be paid for those.

- Get all severance details in writing.

- Evaluate what happened as objectively and calmly as possible.

- Try to learn from the experience.

- Let your colleagues hear from you that you will be leaving. You will want them to know the facts straight from you instead of an embellished version from others.

Cyclist Lance Armstrong was fired from the French racing team Cofidis in 1997, after he began cancer treatment. He was also refused medical coverage and the remainder of his salary. He went on to win the Tour de France seven consecutive times, most recently in 2005.

If you've been downsized, laid off, or just plain fired, the Pink Slip Party may be for you. In addition to the usual party food/drink and small talk, it features recruiters and headhunters looking for new talent, as well as career coaches to help the recently unemployed get back on track.

- Thank those who have been of help to you during your tenure with the company. Putting your appreciation in writing will serve as a permanent record that you acted with responsibility in a difficult situation.

- Accept rejection as a fact of life.

- Realize that whatever led to your being let go has at least two points of view. Try to see the process from the other side.

- Accept part of the blame.

- Think about what you could have done that would have led to another result, and what you will do differently next time.

- Focus on a time when you'll be working again.

- Remember that not learning from the experience will be the worst that can happen.

- Get final employment terms in writing.

- Surround yourself with positive, enthusiastic people.

- Be honest about what happened with future employers.

Leaving Your Job:
Deportment for Departing

- Evaluate your transferable skills and honestly evaluate what you have to offer a new employer.

- Use benefits that may not be available soon. For example, if you have insurance, you may want to schedule a check-up before you change jobs/insurance.

- Look at the experience as a chance to do something you might not otherwise have done.

- Leave on a positive note if at all possible.

- Let clients and customers know you will be leaving.

- Reevaluate your references. Find out whether you will be able to depend on anyone from the company you are leaving for a positive reference.

- Update your resume and get back in the job market as soon as possible.

- Remove personal information from your files and computer.

- Leave your work area in good order.

The term "fire" came to mean being released from one's job back in 1885. It probably came from the word "discharge," which means to fire a gun, and then came to be used simply as to "fire" an employee. Other creative terms include "give one's walking papers" (1825), "get the bounce" (1879), "get the blue envelope" (1927), and "get the pink slip" (1930s).

QUITTING YOUR JOB

Quitting your job is something everyone has to face at one time or another. Make sure that a smooth departure paves the way for future opportunities or at least a good reference at an appropriate time.

What NOT to Do

• Do not think that by leaving you will sever ties entirely—you may think a particular association will never be helpful to you in the future, but people and places from our past have a surprising way of coming back into our lives unexpectedly.

• Do not talk freely about your anticipated move before you are certain of it. Discussing your plans with even one colleague could allow your plans to get back to your supervisor before you are ready to make a decision.

• Do not let your colleagues find out on their own that you are leaving. Tell them, or make an official announcement.

• Do not e-mail your resignation or communicate it by telephone. Your boss deserves to hear face-to-face that you are leaving.

• Do not talk freely about things that have bothered you about your employer.

• Do not act happy to be free of your employer.

• Do not quit your job on an impulse. Have a good, well-considered reason for wanting to go.

It's who you know! Networking is the most effective method to use in looking for a new job.

Leaving Your Job:
Deportment for Departing

- Do not leave things in a mess. Clean out drawers and storage areas for which you are responsible, and, of course, complete all projects before leaving.

- Do not try to take materials with you that are not rightfully yours. Leave the Rolodex and files for the next person to occupy your job, although you will no doubt want to copy information that you have gathered and that will be useful in your new position.

What to Do

- Check your reasons for wanting to leave. Strife with management or a co-worker may not be suitable reasons. You may have the same problem, or worse, at the next place. Sometimes it's better to try to work something out where you are.

- Be very certain that you want to leave your job before tendering your resignation. Once you submit it, it can seldom be taken back.

- Tell your immediate boss first. It is a professional courtesy, plus he or she may want to ask you to reconsider.

- Ask to speak with your boss at a time when others will not be around, and when you can have his or her undivided attention.

- Offer your resignation in written form after you have delivered it verbally. Your company will probably want this for its records.

- Be thoughtful with any comments about why you wish to leave. Venting frustrations may feel good at the time, but it is not wise.

- Be sure to thank your employer for the opportunities he or she has provided during your time there and indicate that you are grateful to the company. Remember that you may need this person as a reference later down the road.

- Understand that your employer may be disappointed or hurt at your leaving. Try not to become involved in emotional discussions about it.

- Give an appropriate amount of notice before you actually leave. Your employer may ask for more or less time, depending on circumstances.

- Let clients and customers know you are leaving the company.

> **"Every job is a self-portrait of the person who does it. Autograph your work with excellence."**
> Unknown